PATRIOTIC SY

MW00764917

The Pledge of Allegiance

Nancy Harris

Heinemann Library
Chicago, Illinois

Photo research by Tracy Cummins and Heather Mauldin
Designed by Kimberly R. Miracle
Maps by Mapping Specialists, Ltd.
Printed and bound in China by South China Printing Company

15 14 13 12 11
10 9 8 7 6 5 4 3

10 Digit ISBN: 1-4034-9378-2 (hc)   1-4034-9385-5 (pb)

Library of Congress Cataloging-in-Publication Data
Harris, Nancy, 1956-
  The pledge of allegiance / Nancy Harris.
     p. cm. -- (Patriotic symbols)
  Includes bibliographical references and index.
  ISBN 978-1-4034-9378-1 (hc) -- ISBN 978-1-4034-9385-9 (pb) 1. Bellamy, Francis. Pledge of allegiance--Juvenile literature. 2. Emblems, National--United States--Juvenile literature. I. Title.
  JC346.H37 2007
  323.6'50973--dc22
                               2006039380

Acknowledgements
The author and publisher are grateful to the following for permission to reproduce copyright material: ©Alamy **p. 12** (Chuck Pefley); ©AP Photo **pp. 6** (Phil Coale), **9** (Koji Sasahara), **11** (The Oklahoman/Steve Sisney), **19** (Starkville Daily News/Brian Loden), **23** (Phil Coale); ©Corbis **pp. 16** (Paul A Souders), **17** (Royalty Free), **20** (Ariel Skelley), **21** (Lorenzo Ciniglio); ©Getty Images **pp. 4** (Royalty Free), **5** (quarter, Don Farrall), **14** (David McNew), **23** (Royalty Free); ©istockphoto **p. 5** (Liberty Bell, drbueller); ©Redux **p. 18** (The New York Times/Andrea Mohin); ©Reuters **pp. 8** (Francois Lenoir), **13** (Paul Hosefros), **23** (Paul Hosefros); ©Shutterstock **pp. 5** (Statue of Liberty, Ilja Mašík), **5** (White House, Uli), **15** (Barry Salmons).

Cover image reproduced with permission of ©Getty Images (Dirk Anschutz). Back cover image reproduced with permission of ©Getty Images (Royalty Free).

Every effort has been made to contact copyright holders of any material reproduces in this book.
Any omissions will be rectified in subsequent printings if notice is given to the publisher.

Contents

What Is a Symbol?

The Pledge of Allegiance is a symbol.
A symbol is a type of sign.

A symbol shows you something.
A symbol can have words.

The Pledge of Allegiance

The Pledge of Allegiance is a special symbol.

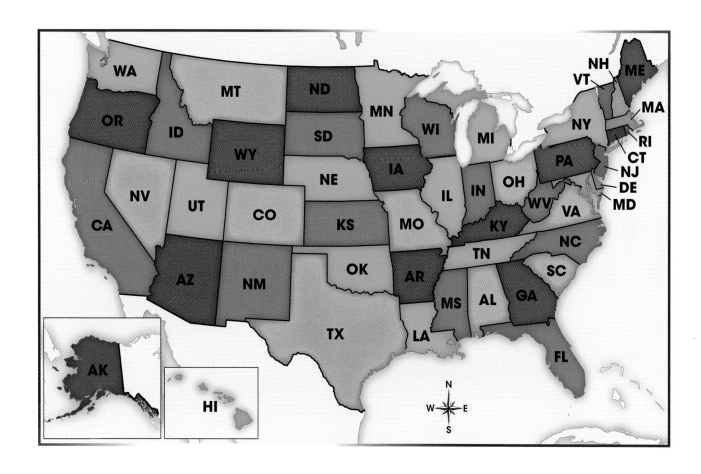

It is a symbol of the United States of America.
The United States of America is a country.

The Pledge of Allegiance is a patriotic symbol.

It shows the beliefs of the United States.
It tells how people support the country.

Words

I Pledge Allegiance to the flag of the United States of America and to the Republic for which it stands, one Nation under God, indivisible, with liberty and justice for all.

The Pledge of Allegiance has special words.

To pledge is to promise something.

The words are a promise to be loyal to the
United States.

To be loyal is to support the country.

To be loyal is to believe in your country.

The Pledge is a symbol of loyalty to the United States.

The American Flag

We pledge allegiance to our country and the American flag.

The flag is a symbol of freedom.

We promise to support freedom.

We promise to support freedom for all people.

What It Tells You

The pledge is a promise to support the United States.

The pledge is a promise to support freedom for all.

Pledge of Allegiance Facts

★ The Pledge of Allegiance was written by Francis Bellamy.

★ In 1954, "under God" was added to the words of the Pledge. No other changes have ever been made to the Pledge.

Timeline

⊕ The Pledge of Allegiance was written in 1892.

Picture Glossary

 **allegiance** loyalty to the place where you live

 **country** an area of land that is ruled by the same leader

 **patriotic** believing in your country

 **symbol** something that stands for something else. Symbols can stand for feelings, places, or objects.

Index

Note to Parents and Teachers

The study of patriotic symbols introduces young readers to our country's government and history. Books in this series begin by defining a symbol before focusing on the history and significance of a specific patriotic symbol. Use the timeline and facts section on page 22 to introduce readers to these non-fiction features.

The text has been carefully chosen with the advice of a literacy expert to enable beginning readers success while reading independently or with moderate support. An expert in the field of early childhood social studies curriculum was consulted to provide interesting and appropriate content.

You can support children's nonfiction literacy skills by helping students use the table of contents, headings, picture glossary, and index.